In The Name of God

HALQEH MYSTICISM

(INTERUNIVERSAL MYSTICISM)

Mohammad Ali Taheri

First published in Farsi (Persian) in 2006

ISBN-10: 1939507103
ISBN-13: 978-1939507105
LCCN: 2013934635

Interuniversal Press

Dedicated to:

My Patient Wife,

Who with Her Care and Tolerance

Aided Me in Accomplishing this

Mission of Great Significance.

Contents

Preface

Iran and The World of Mysticism[1]

In today's world, human beings are subject to a state of unrestraint and confusion, and following that, a deep feeling of emptiness arises within. This feeling results from the lack of spirituality, and expansion of egocentricity in man, which are relentlessly increasing. We also clearly observe the void caused by the absence of feeling God's Presence. At the same time, people's hope for the world of science to make them happy and answer their questions is becoming vain; because science from one hand generates questions and on the other hand, itself is caused as a result of man's raised questions (Science raises questions and questions create science). Consequently, the number of branches of science is increasing each and every day, and the number of man's questions is growing even more rapidly.

---

1. Mysticism or Erfan (Farsi translation for mysticism which is also spelt Irfan, that literally means knowing) is the pursuit of achieving communion with (or conscious awareness of) the Ultimate truth, Divinity, or God. In mysticism this is made possible through direct experience, revelation, or intuitive insight. For detailed explanation please refer to the book "Human from another outlook", the Definition of Erfan, by Mohammad Ali Taheri.

This incremental trend leads the human being to the border of «question crisis», a border at which science can no longer keep up with human to answer their questions. As a result, with human being's progress, the number of their questions reaches the border of infinity, and the hope for a reduction in the number of questions over time becomes impossible.

At such a stage, mankind will become permanently disappointed with science's ability to explain the purpose of the creation of man and the universe, and such disappointment exists even now. Therefore, all nations and ethnicities are working to present what it has been available to them as mysticism and sometimes pseudo-mysticism to the rest of the world. Probably during the course of history, mysticism has never thrived before, to this extent, throughout the world and this indicates human being's inner need for new type of experiences which can be found only in the world of mysticism (Erfan).

Currently, Iran, a formerly well-known base for mysticism, having nurtured numerous mystics, has not thus far been able to present an understandable mystic framework to the world, a framework that everyone can easily understand, obtain, and apply pragmatically. This is true because the era of taking refuge in caves, hanging from wells [undergoing mortification] and the like is long past, and individuals expect to obtain everything easily.

Today's people face a severe lack of time and want to do everything by a schedule so they know exactly what they are going to achieve and how much time is required to achieve it; and they no longer have the required patience to enter into ambiguous and very complicated issues. Additionally, they are in great demand for original, clear and transparent speech.

Say something new to refresh both worlds,
So that it passes beyond both worlds, beyond all limits.
The turn of old sellers has passed away,

We are new sellers and here it is our market.

-Molana Rumi[2]

In addition, the era of vague and mere beautiful speech has passed, and whatever is expressed in words should be demonstrated in practice; specifically, when these words are in the world of mysticism, their practical aspects should definitely be revealed. Otherwise, notes will be merely forms on paper and words will be empty sounds in space. In this era, empty words and notes that do not meet the demands of the suffering and impatient individuals are of no use.

Something should be done from deep inside the soul,
And storytelling does not solve your problem.
A water spring inside the house,
Is better than a river outside.

Today, Iran has become the arena for mysticisms of all nations and ethnicities. Native American, Tibetan, Chinese, Japanese, Indian, Philippine, Vietnamese, and other types of mysticism, even western mysticism speak to us self-righteously and in different forms and colors about Love as if they had been pioneers of the world's mysticism. They offer our own several hundred year-old sayings to us in such decorations as if we had never known *the world of Love (Eshq)* before. Unfortunately in such a situation, Iran's theoretical and practical mysticism is entirely absent; although it is indeed so rich that it can attract and serve the people of the entire world well.

Unfortunately, we are now subject to a kind of «cultural induction» that is far more dangerous than cultural invasion because we are secretly and silently being suggested that we have nothing to say in the world of Erfan and that we need to retreat to other nations; therefore, different techniques from all over the world have been imported into Iran under the guise of

---

2- Molana Jalal-e-Din Mohammad Molavi, also known as Rumi, an Iranian mystic and poet.

mysticism or one of its subsets. However, as it will be discussed later, the definition of mysticism states that Erfan and the world of Love is a world free of tools that cannot include any type of skill or technique.

Hence, those who are not familiar with this definition accept non-mystical concepts as mysticism and are heavily biased toward it. Consequently, our new generation has eventually come to believe that Iran has no presentable mysticism. This point brings pain to the heart of every Iranian who knows at least a few words about Iranian Erfan, or who has heard or read even a few poems by Iranian mystics, and therefore one feels that we have not been good heirs to our rich heritage of ancient Iranian Erfan, and have not succeeded in sufficiently benefiting from it.

Of course, as previously mentioned, this issue results from indifference and low self-esteem on one hand, and lack of an up-to-dated framework for Iran's theoretical and practical Erfan and fresh thoughts on the other. Furthermore, no new action has been taken for presenting our mysticism to the new generation in today's world, and the problems posed by the society against such presentation have cast the veil of obscurity and oblivion over this valuable capital. Here, we understand that the result of the efforts and transcendental revelations (awareness) of all Iranian mystics are left untouched in the libraries and the saying that "what he already had, he kept asking from others"[3] applies to our case.

Today, for the above-mentioned reasons, anybody who masters anything of Iranian mysticism that can be presented to the new generation and the world should take action and be part of this great movement of "promoting Iranian Erfan".

It may be said that all the world's mysticisms want to save the human being from emptiness, so what is the difference between various mysticisms?

3- A poem by Hafez, an Iranian mystic and poet.

The answer is that there is a great difference, which necessitates specialized expert's discussion in this field.

One of these differences is the use of «skills and techniques», which is indeed absent in [original] mysticism. When an individual acquires a capability and power by using a technique, it will be overall attributed to their personal power and proper application of the technique; thus, the individual would suffer from pride, boasting and self-praise. This is the problem infecting today's human being and should be avoided; not simply getting infected by it in another way. In contrast, when this ability is entrusted to him/her through divine grace, the individual cannot regard it as a personal capability; therefore, they will not suffer from false states [such as pride and so on].

Another point is that certain schools of mysticism present and encourage various methods for trespassing individuals' privacy by mind-reading, bewitching or [injuriously] influencing others, reading others' personalities and so on. These people have not considered that such actions are not part of mysticism and do not follow the path of Kamal[4], and can be applied only for obtaining power and dominance over others, and creating multiplicity[5].

Among the many individuals who have been attracted to these schools, maybe no one has asked the questions about how these actions can lead to human Kamal. And this is one of the distinguishing aspects between the Kamal-seeking mysticism which seeks Kamal for individuals and the

---

4- The term Kamal literally means completeness and refers to the human spiritual growth toward completion (perfection). It includes self-realization and self-awareness, meaning clarity of vision about the universe, attaining awareness regarding where we have come from and for what purpose we did so, and also where we are heading. It is attaining possessions which are transportable to the next life (the space-less world) after the physical lifetime on Earth; including perceptions such as «Unity (wholeness) of existence», «magnificence of the Beloved», «the perception of His presence», «purposefulness of creation».

5- For details please refer to principle 3, general principles of the Halqeh mysticism.

power-seeking mysticism which seeks power for them.

A further point is that in these frameworks no border has been defined for the «Negative Network» and the «Positive Network»[6], and they fail to separate the activities of the positive network from those of the negative network. The study and investigation on the origin of the presented powers in certain branches of mysticism reveal that a majority of them belong to the negative network and they are achievable only in that context. For instance, one of the characteristics of the positive network is that it keeps people's right of privacy and their confidentiality (Satar-al-Oyoub); thus, the positive network never offers anyone the possibility to trespass on others' being, read their personalities and unveil their flaws. Such actions are definitely performed through the negative network because «God knows what is truely in the hearts»[7]. Unfortunately, most people are not aware of these issues and [sometimes] even consider such powers as «God-given grants». However, how it can be possible for God -who veils the flaws- to allow human beings to see and reveal one another's flaws?

Another issue here is that mysticism has its own specific language for each nation, which is foreign to other nations and difficult to comprehend. For example, in Iranian Erfan, the Rope (bond) which God stretches out for people, [drinking] wine from the wine-jar of Unity, Saki (spiritual wine server)[8], Shahed[9], Motreb (musician), [spiritual] drunkenness, candle and butterfly, and so on are truly mixed in with our flesh, skin, and bones; we are acquainted with them and they lie deep in our collective unconscious

---

6- For details please refer to principle 29, general principles of the Halqeh mysticism.

7- Quran; Al-e Imran Surah, 119

8- In Iranian mysticism and poems, Saki refers to an individual or a means through which the divine grace and awareness (inspiration, joyfulness and bliss, divine love and affection,…) flows.

9- Means beautiful woman or handsome youth that is sometimes a metaphor for the Creator (God) in mystic language. In Halqeh mysticism shahed also means the state of being an impartial observer.

in such a way that even if we do not know their meanings completely (like all other words which should be decoded and demodulated anew), hearing and reading them still creates a feeling of joy and exultation, the reason for which we do not clearly know; and in the depth of our difficulties we feel cheered up and flourished upon coming across these words, whereas the same words are completely meaningless to a native American, just as their words or phrases would be meaningless to us. For instance, if we hear "pipe with a long stem of unity or peace pipe", we simply laugh.

To summarize the discussion, let us ask the question: why should we ask for something that we already have? Nevertheless, in today's world, mysticism is used as an effective tool for cultural influence, and intense activities are being carried out around the world with this purpose. Mysticism is one means of obtaining credibility and prestige and has attracted the attention of many nations.

«Halqeh Mysticism (Erfan-e Halqeh)» or «Interuniversal[10] Mysticism» that is founded upon Iran's mysticism, seeks to promote it within the framework of «world free of tools»[11]. In the theoretical part of this mysticism, by determining the borders of «positive and negative» networks, and separating «power-based and Kamal-based» pathways, it has been able to present an easy, simple and comprehensively understandable mysticism, reconciling the worlds of religion, mysticism, and science, and resolving

---

10- Interuniversal, in summary, is the perspective of Halqeh mysticism about the universe which includes the ascendance of the human thoughts up to the level of the whole universe. In this regard, Halqeh mysticism desires to pass beyond and above all the ancestral, tribal, racial, national (and so on) limitations, and to reach the perception of the universe through perceiving the Interuniversal Consciousness or Divine Intelligence, and Divine Communal Mercy (the general Divine Grace that includes all human beings without exception and makes the path toward Kamal accessible to everyone). It is believed that without such a holistic perception; one cannot draw an appropriate map or purpose for the pathway of Kamal (spiritual development). Based on Interuniversalism, mankind must expand his thought as vast as the entire existence, viewing life from a wider viewpoint and figuring out his/her own unique position within existence.

11- For details please refer to principle 13, general section of the Halqeh mysticism philosophy.

the existing misunderstandings among them.

In addition, Halqeh mysticism can create practical, rapid, and public accessibility to practical mysticism by connecting (Ettesal) individuals to the network of divine consciousness (Interuniversal Consciousness)[12], and consequently gain unprecedented universal credit for Iran's Erfan.

In this regard and for this grand divine movement, everybody's cooperation and conferment are required, and we hope to enjoy the assistance, guidance and affection of all who are interested in human transcendence and Kamal.

To clarify the different dimensions of Halqeh mysticism, which is an Iranian and Islamic mysticism derived from our culture, principles are presented in two sections, the general and specific principles of Halqeh mysticism.

Please share your suggestions, criticisms, and questions for the further growth of this collection for use in future activities.

Thanks to all who have helped us in this important endeavor.

Wishing you Divine Grace

Mohammad Ali Taheri

12- For details please refer to principles 18 and 19, general section of the Halqeh mysticism philosophy.

And hold fast, all together, to the Rope (bond) which God (stretches out
for you), and be not divided among yourselves.

(Quran; Ale-Imran Surah, 103)

The curls (Halqehes) of alluring chain of the Beloved's hair
is the trap of Love.
The one who is out of this chain
Is disengaged from all these ventures.

-Saadi

Halqeh[1] **Mysticism** (Erfan-e Halqeh) or Interuniversal Mysticism is a
type of mystical exploration and transformation that examines mystical
concepts both in practical and theoretical terms. Since it is inclusive of
all human beings, all people regardless of their race, nationality, religion,
and personal beliefs can accept its theoretical aspects, and experience and
make use of its practical applications.

The general principles are listed and defined as follows:

1- Halqeh: literally means circle. Every Halqeh is a hypothetical circle that has three members. Upon
the formation of the Halqeh, divine grace immediately flows through it and the necessary actions will
take place. Each Halqeh provides us a special facility.

❖ Principle 1

The purpose of this branch of mysticism is to help people reach Kamal[2] and transcendence, a movement from the world of Multiplicity to the world of Unity. In this regard, all efforts are for bringing people close to one another, and avoiding any factor that separates people and creates division amongst them.

❖ Principle 2

The world of Unity is applied to a world that is perceptual (needs to be perceived) in which an individual perceives the Unified Body of the universe [3], and the universe with all its constituents are perceived as divine manifestations. In such a state, individuals consider themselves in connection and unity with all constituents of the universe.

❖ Principle 3

The world of Multiplicity is applied to a world in which individuals are separated from each other to such an extent that the world of each individual is entirely limited to themselves, s/he does not recognize [anyone] outside the self and only takes themselves into account, and is only concerned about maintaining their personal benefits and material and earthly life. This trend finally results in a self-conflict, and personal contradictions reach their maximum level. In the world of Multiplicity, no two people can tolerate each other.

❖ Principle 4

All people can reach an agreement and a common viewpoint on the

Halqeh Mysticism

2- Please refer to footnote 4 in the preface.

3- Such a person comes to this perception that the universe is in fact the unified elements of one body.

intelligence and consciousness governing the universe. After testing and proving [the existence of] this consciousness, they can become aware of the owner of it, who is God, so that this becomes the common meeting point of all human beings' beliefs and gains consolidation and strength. Therefore, the common intellectual factor among all individuals or in other words, the intellectual infrastructure among all humanity is the governing consciousness of the universe or divine consciousness.

In Halqeh mysticism, this common factor is called the "Network of Interuniversal Consciousness" or "Hooshmandi".

❖ Principle 5

The universe has been created from motion; thus, all its various manifestations have also resulted from motion. For the reason that any manifestation resulting from motion is illusory, the physical world is also virtual; in addition, because any motion requires a motive force [to cause the movement] and a directing factor [to give it a direction], the factor governing the universe is awareness or the consciousness governing it, which we call the "Network of Interuniversal Consciousness". Therefore, the physical world has no external existence and is a virtual image of another truth. It is in essence created from awareness, and its constituents are as follows:

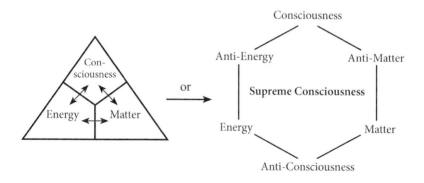

Considering that the consciousness governing the universe must itself have been created from somewhere and governed by [another] source, we acknowledge this source as the owner (master) of this consciousness and we call it "God".

❦ Principle 6

Relation of truth to illusion:

$$\frac{\text{Truth}}{\text{Illusion}} = \frac{\text{Me}}{\text{My image in the mirror}} = \frac{\text{Interuniversal Consciousness}}{\text{The universe}} = \frac{\text{God}}{\text{Interuniversal Consciousness}} = \frac{\text{God}}{\text{Divine manifestations}}$$

❦ Principle 7

Imagining God with multiple fragmented pieces is impossible and He is in unity and integration; thus, His manifestations (the universe) must also be in unity and integration; nothing can be added to or subtracted from them. As a result, the universe is integrated, and all its constituents are related to each other and are considered as one Unified Body [or unified elements of one body].

$$\frac{\text{Beloved (God)}}{\text{Manifestations of the Beloved (God)}} \rightarrow \frac{\text{His unity and integration}}{\text{Integration of His manifestations}} \rightarrow \frac{\text{His limitlessness}}{\text{Limitlessness of His image}} \rightarrow \frac{\text{His flawlessness}}{\text{Flawlessness of His manifestations}}$$

❦ Principle 8

Assuming limitation for God is impossible, and His existence is limitless. Therefore, His manifestations must also be limitless. As a result, the universe is limitless.

20

Principle 9

Due to the infinity of His manifestations, the dipolar world (the world that man knows and he spends his earthly life in) cannot be His only manifestation; therefore, this world is merely one of the worlds of existence. In other words, the universe is itself composed of infinite unknown parallel worlds. Therefore:

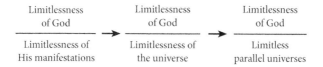

$$\frac{\text{Limitlessness of God}}{\text{Limitlessness of His manifestations}} \rightarrow \frac{\text{Limitlessness of God}}{\text{Limitlessness of the universe}} \rightarrow \frac{\text{Limitlessness of God}}{\text{Limitless parallel universes}}$$

Principle 10

The physical world has no constant form and appearance. Every observer sees it in a different way depending on the observer's movement speed in space and the eye's frequency. If no observer exists, no physical world will exist. Every eye (human, animal, and so on) is designed in such a way as to reveal the universe in a particular appearance to its owner, and it is the eye that reports to its owner (the observer) the vitual image caused by the movement of particles. If an eye frequency is infinite, it will observe nothing in the universe.

Principle 11

The human being is the observer of the universe, and the univerese is the observer of the human being. No reality is lost in the universe, and it acts like a huge memory that records and holds all events within it, eternally.

❖ Principle 12

Individuals' beliefs are divided into two sections, infrastructure and super-structure. The infrastructure is the common intellectual part shared among all individuals. As it is proved in the theoretical and practical parts of Halqeh mysticism, the intellectual infrastructure is the divine consciousness or intelligence governing the universe, which is utilized in this branch of mysticism. The intellectual superstructure includes the instructions of religions and different definitions and paths for man to attain transcendence. The intellectual superstructure in turn can be divided into two sections; general and specific.

In Halqeh mysticism, the human being's intellectual infrastructure is primarily examined, and some definitions are proposed for the common intellectual superstructure. Halqeh mysticism has no interaction or interference with the specific intellectual superstructure that includes various rituals, ceremonies, and beliefs. In fact, Halqeh mysticism proves the [existence of] divine consciousness in theory and practice, and in this way proves the existence of the owner of this consciousness, God. This mysticism indeed results in practical theology.

❖ Principle 13

The human being is always faced with two steps: the step of Wisdom and the step of Love.

The step of Wisdom is the world of science and knowledge, technique, method and skill, advice and counsel, reasoning, arguments, and rationalization diligence and effort, and so on, and in general it is within a scope called the "World of Tools". The step of Love is the world of joyfullness and bliss, enthusiasm and passion, amazement and bewilderment, rapture, sacrifice and affection, and so on, and in general it is the framework and scope which we call the "Tool-less (Free of Tools) World."

Therefore, considering the above-mentioned definitions, Halqeh mysti-

Halqeh Mysticism

cism is composed of two parts, theoretical and practical. The theoretical part is based on the step of Wisdom, and the practical part takes place on the step of Love and uses absolutely no tools.

✤ Principle 14

Practical mysticism consists of understanding the truth of the universe through revelation and direct (witness-like) intuition. In other words, it is a world without the tools of Wisdom, and its perceptions must be obtained through connection and communication with the divine, and receiving awareness.

✤ Principle 15

The step of Wisdom is the basis of understanding the step of Love, and all human conceptions are achieved on this step. Since all conclusions are obtained on the step of Wisdom, Kamal cannot be attained without the step of Wisdom. Thus, the steps of Love and Wisdom are correlated.

✤ Principle 16

A rational man [a person merely on the step of wisdom] falls in love, and a person in love becomes wise; Love is the bridge between partial intellect and the 'whole' wisdom. In other words, the 'whole' wisdom cannot be understood through partial intellect unless one [is being shifted from the step of Wisdom and] stands on the step of Love.

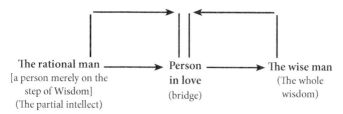

The rational man ⟶ Person ⟶ The wise man
[a person merely on the   in love   (The whole
step of Wisdom]   (bridge)   wisdom)
(The partial intellect)

❦ Principle 17

In heavenly (spiritual) matters, surrendering and submission are the determining factors, whereas in earthly (worldly) matters, effort and endeavor are. The worldly issues themselves are a function of free will and predestination.

Predestination is the collection of all the events beyond the control and free will of human being, which determines man's progress. Predestination is divided into two sections:

➤ Known (verifiable) predestination: a kind of predestination in which the reason for occurrences can be discovered, such as earthquakes, which occur because of the increased pressure of gasses in the Earth's layers and the level of faults' resistance and so on.

➤ Unknown predestination: a kind of predestination with completely unknown and intractable reasons for occurrences, such as a child's choice of being born to particular parents or in a particular birthplace. Unknown predestination is a factor that makes the dipolar world unpredictable and makes the philosophy of man's progress meaningful. Otherwise, all incidents would be calculable and predictable, and the philosophy of man's creation would be meaningless.

❦ Principle 18

To utilize the practical part of Halqeh mysticism, there is a need to connect to (establish Ettesal with) the various Halqehes of the Interuniversal Consciousness network. These connections are the inseparable and integral principle of this branch of mysticism, and in order to fulfill each concept of practical mysticism, a special Halqeh and its related «protective shield (layer)[4]» are required.

Connection (Ettesal) is presented to two groups, users [students, pa-

---

4- Please refer to principle 44, general priciples of Halqeh mysticism.

Halqeh Mysticism

tients,..] and trainers (masters), by means of vouchsafing and in exchange for signing the related text of oath. This entrusting is carried out by a center which controls and directs the Halqeh mysticism's conduct.

❖ Principle 19

There are two general types of Ettesal to the network of Interuniversal Consciousness:

A- Individually or Personal Type (And your Lord says: "Call on Me (Od'uni); I will answer you/your prayer." Quran; Ghafir Surah, 60)

In the personal type, an individual, by means of his/her extraordinary and prodigious eagerness and enthusiasm (Eshtiyaq)[5], becomes connected to the Interuniversal Consciousness. To establish such an Ettesal, a prodigious Eshtiyaq is necessary. Except for that, there is no definition for this way of Ettesal.

B- Collective or Common Type ("And hold fast, all together, to the Rope (bond) which God (stretches out for you), and be not divided among yourselves" Quran; Ale-Imran Surah, 103)

In the collective way, with the assistance of an individual who serves as a connector, one becomes present in the Halqeh ([symbolic] circle) of Unity. Every Halqeh, as shown in the figure, has three members:

(1) The Interuniversal Consciousness

(2) The person who serves as a connector [Me]

(3) The person who is about to be connected [You]

Upon the formation of the Halqeh, divine grace immediately flows through it, and the desired tasks -within the framework of this mysticism- are fulfilled through formation of different types of Halqeh. For a Halqeh

---

5- Please refer to principle 32, general priciples of Halqeh mysticism.

General Principles

to be formed, the presence of the three aforementioned members is sufficient; in such case, the fourth member will be God (Allah or the Creator).

In Halqeh mysticism, Ettesal is established based on the common or collective way and by formation of the related Halqeh, divine grace flows through it. The formation of Halqeh is illustrated in the following figure:

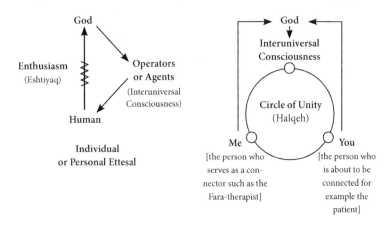

❧ Principle 20

The grace of the Halqeh of Unity is a result of the blessing of closeness and unity of at least two people, and anywhere that at least two people come together in this Halqeh, the third and fourth members will be Holy Spirit (network of Interuniversal Consciousness) and God, respectively.

❧ Principle 21

To perform therapy (Faradarmani[6], Psymento-therapy[7] and so on), the

6- Faradarmani is a subdivision of Halqeh mysticism, and is one of the Halqehs which makes certain facilities available to us. Faradarmani is considered as an alternative and complementary medical treatment and is totally based on mysticism. in this type of therapy, the patient becomes connected (Ettesal) to the Interuniversal Consciousness via Fara-therapist. Faradarmani is founded by Mohammad Ali Taheri (The author) and it is applied for treating physical, psycheal, psychosomatic, and mentosomatic diseases (For details please refer to the book "Human From Another Outlook" and "Faradarmani", by the same author).

7- Psymento-therapy is the practical application of Psymentology (Interuniversal mind-Psychol-

number of people, either the therapists or patients, is not a determining factor because the therapy is entirely performed by divine Interuniversal Consciousness.

✤ Principle 22

The only condition for being present in the Halqeh of Unity is "observing" (being an impartial observer or spectator). An observer (witness) is a person who observes and has no judgment during the observation. S/he keeps all the occurrences during their presence in the Halqeh under observation, without any interpretation, pre-assumption or judgment while observing (saves all contemplations and interpretations for when he comes out of the Halqeh).

✤ Principle 23

When an individual has a request, s/he asks that directly from God ("We ask help -for each and everything- only and absolutely only from You" Quran; Faatihah Surah, 5), but receives the answer through the network of Interuniversal Consciousness (Hand of God, Holy Spirit, Gabriel, and so on).

God

The network of Interuniversal Consciousness
(Hand of God, Holy Spirirt, Gabriel, and so on)

Human

ogy) founded by Mohammad Ali Taheri. (For details please refer to the books "Psymentology" and "Non-organic Beings", by the same author).

✥ Principle 24

A Rind individual is someone who considers and pays attention to both reality and the truth. In Halqeh mysticism, based on the Rind creed, neither is reality sacrificed for the sake of truth, nor is the truth sacrificed for the sake of reality. The Rind is a person who searches for truth in reality and vice versa; in other words, s/he can see both reality and truth.

✥ Principle 25

All the individuals' capabilities are awarded to them as trustees by divine grace in the Halqeh of Unity of the network of Interuniversal Consciousness, and no one has the right to attribute that to him/herself. Every action that results in ego, polytheism, generation of separation and multiplicity, and mental deviations that distract the individuals' attention from the path of Kamal and genuine clairvoyance (which means clearly seeing, understanding and perceiving the universe) is severely denounced.

✥ Principle 26

Nobody has the right to introduce this Ettesal under any title other than the network of Interuniversal Consciousness or divine consciousness; otherwise, it is considered others' deceit, deviating people from the way to God, and misleading them toward "anything other than God, or instead of Him". Also, anything that one may use to show off or aggrandize the self, or anything that leads to egocentricity and claiming superiority over others is a clear example of deviation (Principal of avoiding "I am better than others" [8]).

8- Quran; Al-Araf Surah: 12

Halqeh Mysticism

✥ Principle 27

Any path that the human being follows in metaphysical issues can be applied in two dimensions, power or Kamal. Halqeh mysticism does not heed the pathways toward power[9] and only the Kamal pathway is considered worthwhile.

✥ Principle 28

The true God-given grant to the human being [vs. supernatural powers] is the collection of things that can take people to Kamal, that is, only the awareness and perceptions regarding the potential divine ability [embedded in man]. In other words, on the path to Kamal nobody is asked to state their powers. On the contrary, they are asked about the awareness and perceptions they have obtained.

✥ Principle 29

All the metaphysical awareness and information obtained by an individual comes from either the "Positive Network" or the "Negative Network."

Information from the positive network guides man toward Kamal and facilitates his path in reaching oneness and unity with the universe. This guidance results in inner happiness, calmness, and the like.

Information that provides a means for showing off, attaining personal interests, gaining dominance and influence over others, mind-reading, and all information that contradicts God's divine justice and His fault-veiling (covering of defects), anything that violates man's freedom of

---

9- Power in all its forms is perishable and wastes a human lifetime.

choice, personal privacy and confidentiality, and generates multiplicity, all come from the negative network. The positive network NEVER provides such information. Among the outcomes of using -knowingly or unknowingly- the information from the negative network is feeling anxious and restless, depressed and disappointed, sad or lonely and the like. In addition, all the information that generates fear and apprehension, worrying and anxiety, disappointment and despair, sorrow and grief, and depression, definitely comes from the negative network (whether received in sleep or waking).

Principle 30

Individuals need awareness and information of the positive network to move toward Kamal. Thus, if this awareness is received, hiding and not presenting it will lag people in their path toward Kamal and increase their risk of falling into the negative network, and this is considered a betrayal against humanity. As a result, a person who has received awareness of the positive network is responsible to present it to the public; otherwise, claiming and pretending to have received awareness is merely an act of deception.

Principle 31

People's innermost secrets kept by God are confidential information, and their disclosure contradicts His justice and covering of defects (Satar-al-Oyoub); thus, people are not allowed to enter this boundary [to know such secrets], and entering it is only possible via the negative network. The positive network does not give anyone such information (principle of "Indeed, He only knows what lies within the hearts")[10].

10- Quran; Al-e Imran Surah, 119.

❖ Principle 32

Enthusiasm (Eshtiyaq)[11] is the only incentive for reaching Kamal, and all the awareness (intuitions) that an individual receives is the reward of his/her enthusiasm. [Eshtiyaq is the currency of the world of Kamal, as in this world the most enthusiasts are indeed the wealthiest of all.]

❖ Principle 33

Submission or surrendering in Halqeh is the only condition for the fulfillment of the related Halqeh; otherwise, one must use his personal or individual abilities that are significantly limited.

❖ Principle 34

In Halqeh mysticism, human-related factors such as personal characteristics, geographical and climatic conditions, personal or individual capabilities and facilities and the like, have no role in establishing Ettesal and receiving metaphysical awareness.

These irrelevant factors include the following:

➢ Gender, age, nationality, talent, education, knowledge, type of thinking, beliefs, mystical and spiritual experience, and the like.

➢ Undergoing mortification, strenuous self-discipline, physical exercise, type of nutrition, and the like.

➢ Endeavour, effort, struggle, determination and the like.

➢ Imagination and mental visualization, mantra and chanting, using signs and symbols, prompting suggestion, inculcation and repetition, con-

---

11- An inner burning desire for discovering the truths of existence and becoming closer to God.

centration, and the like.

➤ Numerology, astrology, the position of the stars, the individual's date of birth, and he like.

⟨⟨⟩⟩ Principle 35

Every human being -regardless of race, nationality and religion- seeks transformation and accepts Kamal, and can be on the direct path [to God].

⟨⟨⟩⟩ Principle 36

Considering that Divine Consciousness requires no supplement, nothing can be added to it under any name or label. This can easily be proven; because by removing such added factor, it will be clearly observed that the Halqeh of Unity continues working, and this disgraces the heretics and deceivers. Such characteristic lies at the heart of this relationship to distinguish right from wrong. In this regard, there is absolutely no room for any personal alteration [in the original concepts], and this only reveals the individual's desire to show off, brag and boastfully aggrandize the self.

⟨⟨⟩⟩ Principle 37

The 'thought' is important, not its 'owner' (principle of originality of thought).

⟨⟨⟩⟩ Principle 38

All of the human being's selections should be done via investigating the [various] thoughts (principle of "those who listen to other's speech and follow the best of it"[12]).

❖ Principle 39

The universe has been created purposefully. Therefore, it should follow a grand [purposeful] plan, and it is impossible for its owner (God) to take useless and futile actions.

❖ Principle 40

Therapy is an experimental method for mystical perception of Kamal used for reaching the following goals:

➤ Becoming practically familiar with the consciousness governing the universe (divine consciousness or Interuniversal Consciousness)

➤ Becoming free from being a captive of "self"

➤ Serving people and performing practical worship

➤ Knowing one's inner treasure and spiritual capabilities

➤ Philosophical anthropology (as a part of knowing the self)

➤ Increasing closeness with others and providing the possibility of unity

❖ Principle 41

"Faradarmani" is the name of [one of] the therapeutic branches in this mystical school. This name was chosen to represent the interuniversalistic viewpoint of this school regarding the human being.

12- Quran; Al-zomar Surah, 18.

❧ Principle 42

Interuniversalism is a [meta-holistic] way of viewing the human being that views human being in the breadth and vastness of the universe. In this viewpoint, the human being consists of different bodies [such as the physical body, psycheal body or psyche, mental body (Zehn or Mind), astral body, and others], energy transformers [namely known as Chakra], energy channels [like those of limited, restricted or the fourteen non-physiological channels in the body as investigated and studied in acupuncture], energy fields [such as polarity field, bio-plasma field and so on], cellular consciousness, molecular frequency, and an infinite number of other unknown constituents[13].

❧ Principle 43

Practicing this therapy carries absolutely no negative karma or reaction for the individual, and there is no need to ask for God's permission, because it is only carried out by the divine consciousness and not by the therapist[14].

❧ Principle 44

[The ability to carry out] therapy is vouchsafed to the individual by completing a written text of oath, pledging to make positive and humanitarian use [of the related Halqeh], and starts upon receiving the protective shield

---

13- According to Interuniversalism, the definition of illness is: "Any disorder, obstruction, damage, and imbalance in any of the infinite elements and constituents of the human being."
14- Man -the noblest of noble creatures, for which God glorified Himself for his creation- is not worthy of pain and illness. Thus, the effort to free himself from pain and suffering and humiliation not only causes no negative Karma (reaction), but is also a part of his mission, especially because a number of pains and illnesses are a result of the individual's life style, mental attitude, false beliefs, and, most important of all, falling away from Divine (Communal) Mercy.

(layer)[15]. This layer [under the control of the Interuniversal Consciousness] protects the therapist [and the patient during treatment] against "the emissions of defective cellular consciousness," "other negative emissions," and "infiltration by Non-organic Beings."[16]

✥ Principle 45

Considering that therapy is carried out by the divine consciousness, the therapist has no right to consider any type of disease as incurable.

✥ Principle 46

In the view that the network of Interuniversal Consciousness is the collection of consciousness governing the universe, and is neither matter nor energy, the dimensions of time and space do not govern it; thus, treatment is possible in place or at long distances.

✥ Principle 47

Since therapy is carried out by the divine consciousness; therefore, therapists cannot attribute anything [power of healing] to themselves.

15- The protective layer is made of awareness and its form and manner is unique for each individual similar to his/her fingerprint; hence, there is no possibility for two individuals to have the same protective layer.

16- The term "Non-organic Beings" is applied to beings that are void of any organic or material aspect, whose unidentified form is not amassed with any atoms or molecules. According to the "non-organic viruses theory" mankind is encountered with viruses that could affect his mind, body and psyche; infiltrate in man's diverse existing constituents and software-based data files, having them contaminated with parasites and derangement, and consequently bring about all kinds of hallucinations, abnormal behaviors and unusual drives. (For details on non-organic beings please refer to the book "Non-organic Beings," by the same author.)

In Halqeh mysticism, the main path is Tariqat[17], which is the path of practice on which truth and religion are understood. Finally, all three coincide and correspond to each other. This movement can happen as per below figure, which means that, in practice, human being understands the application of religion[18] and also achieves the truth[19].

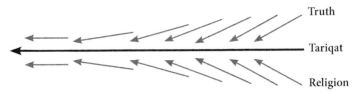

Truth

Tariqat

Religion

It is clear that the human being, due to the structure of his existence, re-

Halqeh Mysticism

17- The path of life is tariqat if it leads toward Kamal. In this particular sense, tariqat is the path of mystical movement. For an individual to transform during their non-mystical life and move toward Kamal, a stimulus is needed. This stimulus awakens the individual who was accustomed to the routine life and opens a valuable and new horizon for them. Thus, the individual enters (mystical) tariqat only after receiving such awareness. This stimulus can be "nature," "religion," or "truth" (For details please refer to the book "Human and Insight," by the same author).

18- The transformation and growth of an individual on the Kamal path require following the methods and observing the commands provided by God as revealed through thousands of prophets and leaders. Undoubtedly, the grand divine plan for human creation will not be effective without these messengers' messages. Therefore, religions and decoding their mysteries have special importance.

Every religion has two inner and outer dimensions, the external one being called "religion (shariat)." Typically, before any person achieves the truth of religion, s/he confronts with the external part. External religion can motivate the progression to the truth of religion. In any case, religion is a stimulus for entering mystical tariqat. Even someone who follows no particular religion may achieve spiritual awareness during a religious ceremony. This occurs when the celebration makes think and stimulates desire to experience its inner effects (For details please refer to the book "Human and Insight," by the same author).

19- The truth of anything is the Whyness of being, Howness of occurrence, and purpose of being of that thing. In other words, "truth" is the hidden aspect or unseen existence within everything. The only way to achieve truth is to receive awareness and inspirations. Even for someone who has not yet entered the path of mysticism, it is possible to receive inspiration. For such individuals, inspiration could be an important stimulus for starting mystical tariqat (For details please refer to the book "Human and Insight," by the same author).

lies on a kind of action for his transformation and growth in the path of Kamal. These actions have been designed by the omniscient God in His grand design, and He has prepared the ground for the presence of thousands of prophets and messengers who had been sent as messengers to announce the message of warning and glad tidings to Kamal seekers and those on the right path. These messengers have drawn human being to religion and the method of moving on the way toward Kamal.

Specific Principles
of the Halqeh Mysticism

The specific section of Halqeh mysticism is recommended simply for being informed and investigated as the general intellectual superstructure of individuals. Each person is free to accept or reject all or a part of it.

Principle 1

The philosophy of creation is based on a completely purposeful plan and program, and its final goal is Kamal.

Principle 2

Justice is the integral principle in the creation of human being and the universe, and the philosophy of creation is vain and futile without that.

Principle 3

Death is considered movement toward God, which is not fearsome and sorrowful.[1] (principle of "Him, to whom we shall return")[2]

Principle 4

In Halqeh mysticism, prayer is in fact "asking for Kamal and divine love and closeness to Him."

Principle 5

The name of God is placed above all the names, and only He is worth calling and turning to, and its violation is polytheism. (Principle of "avoiding anything other than God or instead of Him")

The most important instances of polytheism include:

➢ Anthropolatry (deification and worship of a human being)

1- For detailed explanation please refer to the book "Human Worldview", the law of birth and death, by Mohammad Ali Taheri.

2- Quran; Al-Baqareh, 62

- Ancestor worship

- Hagiolatry (deification and worship of saints)

- Necrolatry (the worship of the dead)

- Ecclesiolatry (obsessive devotion to ecclesiastical traditions)

- Bibliolatry (excessive adherence to a literal interpretation of books, in particular holy books)

- Self-idolatry

- Worshiping the world

- Worshipping the appearance[3]

The divine consciousness (the Hand of God) is the only mediation between the human being and God, which plays its role of the hand of God in various ways, and is the bridge between the lower world and God.

❖ Principle 6

The universe is a divine manifestation and is caused by divine awareness and consciousness; therefore, human being should respect all its constituents. Desecration and covering the holiness of any constituent of the universe is considered "blasphemy".

❖ Principle 7

Destroying and wasting, and suppressing or inhibiting the growth and

---

3- The world of Erfan is a movement from seeing appearance to seeing substance. Seeing substance is "discovering the ultimate Kamal of everything in the world." When one achieves such Godly vision, they perceive the grandeur of all existence in every constituent of it. Having substance-seeing vision reveals three aspects of everything: appearance, substance, and essence. (For details please refer to the book "Human and Insight," by the same author.)

development of divine manifestations and any constituent of the universe are considered "corruption".

❖ Principle 8

Those who believe in divine unity and, and in the way of achieving that, invite people toward union and reconciliation with the self and the universe are called "monotheists", and those who push others toward separation and multiplicity are called "hypocrites".

❖ Principle 9

In the world of mysticism, sorrow has only one meaning, and that is the sorrow of being separated from the Beloved (God) and one's origin [the potential divine ability embedded in human].

❖ Principle 10

"Him, to whom we shall return"[4] is an inherent movement toward Kamal and means moving from multiplicity to unity, and from being needy to free-of-need. It is composed of various lives (stages), each of which ends with death, and the next life begins. For instance, after dying in this stage[5], the "space-less" stage begins, and after that, the "space-less and timeless" life.

❖ Principle 11

Human beings cannot love God because they cannot understand and

---

4- Ilayhi-Rajeoun, Quran; Al-Baqareh, 156
5- Refers to life on planet Earth with the dimensions of time, space and duality.

perceive Him in any possible way[6]. In fact it is God that loves human beings, and man -His beloved- embraces divine love. Human beings can only love His divine manifestations, that is, manifestations of the universe. After this stage, they are blessed with His divine love.

❖ Principle 12

The human being experiences three different worlds:

1. No-polar world: the only absolute truth, and no human words can describe it. It is indescribable and has no conflict. ("Exalted is He and high above what they describe")[7]

2. Unipolar world: can be described, but has no conflict and lacks the dimensions of space and time.

3. Dipolar world or world of two opposites: everything can be understood through understanding its opposite, such as day and night, bad and good, and so on.

❖ Principle 13

In the view of an observer from the unipolar world, there are no dimensions of space and time; thus, there is no past and future, and the universe has been created and ended in zero seconds. Consequently, information related to the past, present, and future of the world is available to the unipolar world observer. According to this theory, human fate has been determined[8]

6- Perceiving God's essence and nature is not possible as it is beyond human descriptions and definitions. We cannot understand His 'being' because it is completely different from what human knows and understands as 'being' (For details please refer to the book "Human and Insight," by the same author).

7- Quran; Al-Momenoun, 91, Al-Anaam, 100 & Al-Saafaat, 159

8- Because the observer in unipolar world (God) knows the collection of each individual's free

but it has not been imposed on the human being, and whatever exists is the result of human's free will [in the dipolar world]; thus, human beings are not considered weak-kneed puppets[9].

❖ Principle 14

Human beings seek metaphysical issues for two reasons:

a. Obtaining power, for gaining superiority over others, showing off, and theatrics that empowers one's arrogance and selfishness. For instance, violation of an individual's privacy and confidentiality, violation of individual sanctity (Home of God) like mind-reading and trespassing on others' being (bewitching), violation of divine justice like astrology and predicting the future, violation of God's defect-covering attribute such as telling people's personalities and revealing their defects, violation of human free will, and the like.

b. Obtaining Kamal, which (in this stage of living on the earth) means perceiving the potential divine ability (the origin) [embedded in human] and the main mission of the human being that is moving from multiplicity to unity, understanding the unity (oneness) of the universe, attaining enlightenment which means clear-sightedness, and clarity of knowing, understanding, and perceiving the universe, and understanding the goal of the transcendent creation (perception of the potential divine ability).

Halyeh Mysticism

---

will, his/her choices, actions,… and their ultimate fates.

9- For instance, based on my free will, I might choose to sit down right now; however, the observer from the unipolar world, due to the lack of time and space, has already seen me sit down in zero seconds, and knows exactly what I will be doing without having imposed any of my actions or choices on me.

Human being in their bodies can only perceive their potential divine ability and are not capable of actualizing it (manifesting it). In other words, no one can become God in the [earthly] physical body. Similarly, God creates and human being perceives. Kamal in body means perceiving human being's potential divine ability. These potential perceptions include:

➢ Perception of "And I (God) breathed into him of My spirit"[10] or "Ana-al-Haqq (I am the Truth (God)"[11] and that He is in the center of our existence (perception of 'The House Of God'[12])

➢ Perception of the wholeness (unity) and the unified body of the universe (divine manifestations)[13]

➢ Perception of the intelligence, grand plan and purposefulness of the universe.

➢ Perception of the flawless "magnificence of the Beloved" (No lover can find any defect in the beauty of his/her beloved.)[14]

10- Quran; Al-hijr, 29

11- This legendary statement apparently led to Mansour Hallaj's -a Persian Sufi- long trial that consequently earned his public execution and martyrdom.

12- Please refer to principle 19, specific section of Halqeh mysticism

13- Perception of the unity (wholeness) governing the universe and that all the particles of universe are in close cohesion, connection and communication with each other is one of the objectives of the world of Erfan. In fact, the universe is integrated and unified; no constituent can exist without the existence of others. Yet the mystic sees this from another point of view, as he sees the universe as the manifestation and the image of the Beloved (God).

14- The Leyli and Majnoon story, a deep love story by the Persian poet Nezami Ganjavi, teaches this lesson clearly to man. In the story, their love became a word of mouth and everyone assumed how beautiful Leyli must have been to have made Majnoon so crazy for her love, to such a level that he wandered about in the plains and deserts. Therefore, everybody was curious to see her, and finally the king summoned Leyli to his palace. He wanted to see her, face to face, to see the beauty that had created such a great love. However, when the king finally met Leyli he was amazed to find her quite an ordinary girl. Therefore, he told her, "Then it is you that have caused Majnoon to madly wander about in the deserts, but you are not prettier than the others?!" In response, Leyli unveiled the great truth: "It is the way Majnoon perceives me that has indeed caused such a passionate love and it is his loving eyes that cannot see my flaws". Someone who has such eyes as Majnoon's can pass through both worlds easily as he cannot see any fault in them.

Specific Principles

➤ Perception of "the presence of God"[15] and reaching the status of having no Qibla.[16] (So wherever you might turn, there is the Image of God)[17]

✦ Principle 16

There is an opposing force against moving toward Kamal.

✦ Principle 17

Worshipping means "being at the service" and fulfilling one's mission as a worshipper. There are two types of worship: theoretical worship and practical worship. Theoretical worship is to have verbal communication with God, and practical worship is to serve God. Since God does not have the slightest need of any of our actions, we can merely serve His manifestations. As a result, practical worship is being at the service of the universe, which is, serving people, nature, and so on.

✦ Principle 18

Worship motivation is divided into three types:

➤ Worship of so-called slaves or worshiping out of fear (of death, the grave, hell, and so on)

➤ Worship of mercenaries or worship out of greed for wages and re-

15- The ardor and yearning of His lovers for His union, brings about incomprehensible exaltation. In this phase of life, [the experience of] joining Him is indeed the perception of His "Presence", higher than which a human cannot experience. Therefore, while we are within our physical body, the maximum level of union with God is reaching the perception of His presence. There is no accurate description for this, because it is taking place at the step of Love in a world that is 'free of tool', therefore this concept is purely perceptual [such as the taste of an apple]. Nevertheless, it is rather 'witnessing His presence,' not the theoretical knowledge of it.
16- Qibla is the direction in Mecca to which Muslims turn for praying.
17- Quran; Baqareh, 115

Halqeh Mysticism

wards (heaven, houris[18], and so on)

> Worship of sincere people or worship out of Divine love

Each person's type of worship and desire depends on the level of their understanding and perception from God and, like a child who prefers a lollipop to a world of awareness; a person may prefer a houri to Divine Love.

In Halqeh mysticism, worshipping out of Divine Love is desired.

Principle 19

"Beitollah" (The House Of God) refers only to the human being, given that it is the only place into which God has breathed His spirit ("And I (God) breathed into him of My spirit"); therefore, approaching human boundaries should be performed with complete [inviolability and] holiness, and no human being is allowed to violate others' privacy.[19]

Principle 20

Individuals' efficiency and superiority are determined, in practice, and in exchange of ideas. Therefore, anyone who says s/he is better than others reveals his/her inexperience and evil. (Principle of "I am better than others")

Principle 21

The [earthly] world is where reality and truth join. Reality is something that has taken place, has happened or has been created, and truth is the Whyness of being (Howness of occurrence), purpose of being (the hid-

18- Beautiful maidens that in Muslim belief live with the blessed in paradise.
19- Anyone who reaches such perception has indeed reached the perception of "Ana-al-Haqq" and is considered an intimate of the "Beitollah."

den aspects of reality) and quality of occurrence; or the hidden, inner, and natural purpose for reality.

⟨❦⟩ Principle 22

[Final stage of] Zekr or chant has passed the stage of "mantra and word or phrase repetition"[20], and reached the definition of "His memory"[21]. After that, it has been promoted to mean "sense of His presence"[22] because "memory" applies to one who is absent, but He is present.

⟨❦⟩ Principle 23

Perception and enhancement of the quality of calling His name passes through the following stages:

"Except God" → "God" (verbal) → "God" (mental; remembers an absent one) → "God" (heartfelt)[23] → "God" (wholehearted or existential) and finally to → "sense of His presence (nameless God)"

20- Verbal Zekr: such a chant is on the step of Wisdom and is mere utterance of words or phrases.

21- Mental Zekr: when verbal chant is upgraded, it is converted into the mental form. In this case, when chanting, the chanter has presence of mind, but his/her chant merely remembers an "absent" one. This means that, first, s/he is remembering God only while chanting, and, second, when remembering God, s/he feels a distance between himself and God, which leads to feeling very little familiarity and proximity with Him.

22- Existential or wholehearted Zekr: Such a perception -praising God on the step of Love- is indescribable in which the person finds himself floating in His divine love. When a person comes to understand the profound truth of monotheism, all monotheistic chants are established in him and engraved on the Axis of Existence of the person, which is called an "existential chant." The existential chant is "adjusting existence around the axis of Kamal" and it will also paint its own color on one's external works. In fact, one's Axis of Existence affects his tongue, eyes, and ears; therefore, even the tongue, eyes and ears of such a person are themselves chanters. This person's eyes will see a manifestation of God in every creature, his ears will hear the beauty of sounds in the world, and his tongue will reflect the Kamal of the beauty of his existence. (For details please refer to "Human Insight" by the same author)

23- Such chant is on the step of Love; however, it is not permanent and is sometimes experienced.

Principle 24

The human being's motivation for positive deeds is to reach Kamal; therefore, there is no obligation on God or people.

Principle 25

God's satisfaction rests in human beings' attempt to reach Him.

Principle 26

In earthly life, the position of "the peaceful" is the highest position that individuals can attain, and "peace-bringing acts" refers to all the actions that bring people closer to peace. The peaceful individuals are those who have reached peace, and this peace includes:

➤ Peace toward one's self

➤ Peace toward the universe

➤ Peace toward God

➤ Peace toward others

Peace toward others is the most difficult part of this peace and is considered the main passage of Halqeh mysticism. The reason for choosing therapy as the starting point for one's exploration and transformation has been to become close to others, understand human misery, and reach the point where people deserve empathy; thus attain a better peace (toward others).

Principle 27

Patience means not dictating to the passage of time [relinquishing control] and not imposing force on time[24]. Therefore, a patient individual is a person who does not dictate and mandate time [and is coherent and symphase with it]. (Symphases with time is a necessary condition for receiving awareness.)

❖ Principle 28

Since the philosophy of human creation has been purely to achieve Kamal and move from the world of multiplicity to unity, and this progress is justifiable based on human free will, therefore all the individual's movements should result from his/her thinking and reasoning, so that they can accept their own responsibility. Thus, such a movement cannot be the product of anything except human free will, and any factor such as astrology and the like that compromises and deprives an individual of their free will, turning them into puppets or tools without authority, is disapproved. In other words, moving toward Kamal cannot be the result of working with numbers (numerology) and consigning matters to anything outside human free will.

❖ Principle 29

Worldly affairs; worldly laws[25].

❖ Principle 30

Do not choose anything for others that you would not choose for yourself.

24- Time, as an intelligent constituent of the universe, reacts against man's force and dictatorship; for instance, when a person wishes time to go by fast, it seems to be passing very slowly or not passing at all, and vice versa. However, a transcendent person is submissive to time and is symphasic with; not wishing it to go fast or slow. (For details please refer to the book "Human Worldview", lack of knowledge, understanding and perception of time, by the same author)

25- Please refer to principle 17, general section of Halqeh mysticism philosophy.

❖ Principle 31

[Qualitative] judgment is only for God[26].

❖ Principle 32

Perceiving the insight of rituals and ceremonies is superior to [the outward performance of] rituals and ceremonies. No ceremony is valuable without apprehending its insight[27].

❖ Principle 33

Religion is a collection of targeted rules and regulations for human beings and societies, which -based on theosophy and the divine intelligence and consciousness- is descended to man for his transcendence on the path of Kamal. Religion is for understanding the essentials of the human existence, and removing both hidden and apparent obstacles in his path of transcendence.

❖ Principle 34

To reach Kamal and transcendence, man needs "guidance mediators". Everything -people, animals, plants, and inanimate things- that assist human beings in any possible way to identify and perceive the laws governing the universe performs this role. In addition, "religious mediators" refer to individuals who due to their unique characteristics (in this arena) have striven to decode awareness, convert it to simple and applied language,

---

26- Qualitative judgment is actually a privilege reserved for God. In presence of God, everyone is valued according to his own rank, but humankind always judges quantitatively (for details please refer to the book "A collection of articles", what is oppression, by the same author.
27- Ceremonies have both appearance (reality) and truth that will not be useful if one does not pay attention to both.

and transfer it to others. They are teachers and distinguished models for humanity who point toward unity.

✤ Principle 35

Every action that diverge an individual from Kamal is considered a sin and any action that brings him closer to Kamal, a virtue.

Finally, because all the above-mentioned points within the mystical framework can be stated as constant principles in the philosophy, the ensuing books will include other principles for use as a reference for the entire discussion.

Printed in Great Britain
by Amazon

77359799R00031